Tigers once roamed over most of Asia. Some trekked over the frozen north, others climbed the jagged mountains of central Asia, and many crept through the hot, humid jungles of the south. Tigers of each region are recognized as different types, or *subspecies*. Six of the subspecies are shown here.

No matter where tigers live, humans have always been the tiger's chief enemy. People have killed so many tigers that two of the subspecies on these pages are extinct, and several others may soon follow. All tigers are considered endangered. The light green areas of the map show where tigers once lived. The smaller blue areas show where they now live.

Because of conservation efforts, th are now about 4,000 Bengal tigers India. It was long considered a ma of manhood to kill a tiger. Young princes were expected to kill their first tiger by the age of or 12. It was not unusual f a maharajah to kill hundr of tigers in his lifetime.

BENGAL TIGER
Panthera tigris tigris

CASPIAN TIGER
Panthera tigris virgata

The Caspian tiger is now extinct. In 1964, there were 80 to 100 of them in northern Iran—a small portion of their former large territory.

The Siberian tiger is the largest of all living tigers. It lives in a cold climate and has very thick fur to keep it warm. Its pale color makes it hard for prey animals to see this large predator in the snows of Siberia. Between 250 and 430 Siberian tigers may still live in the wild.

SIBERIAN, OR AMUR, TIGER
Panthera tigris altaica

South China tigers once lived in most parts of China. Today, only 30 to 80 of these tigers remain in the wild.

SOUTH CHINA TIGER
Panthera tigris amoyensis

SUMATRAN TIGER
Panthera tigris sumatrae

JAVAN TIGER
Panthera tigris sondaicus

There are about 400 Sumatran tigers. They live in dense, tropical jungle on the island of Sumatra, south of the Asian continent. Sumatran tigers are smaller than other tigers. Javan tigers, from the same part of the world, have been extinct since 1976.

The body of a tiger is like a deadly weapon. It has the quickness and strength to take down animals twice its size. It has long, razor-sharp claws for grabbing its prey, and it has enormous teeth, which can easily kill large animals.

A tiger is also very quiet. It can sneak up on its prey without being seen or heard. Its stripes help it to do this, because they make it easier for the tiger to hide.

Another special thing about tigers' stripes is that you can tell one tiger from another by its stripes! On these pages you will have a chance to discover this for yourself.

A tiger's stripes blend perfectly with the dry grass. Tigers also hide well in the dark jungle, where the stripes look just like streaks of shadow and sunlight.

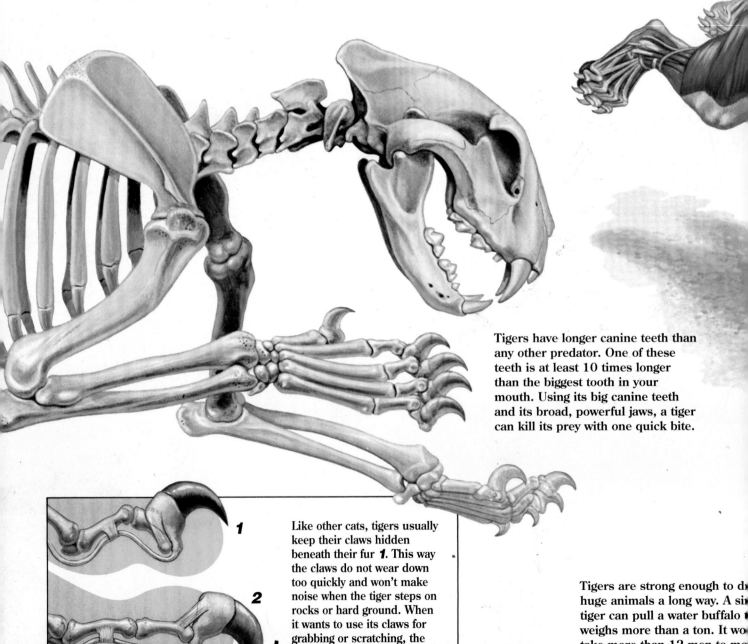

Tigers have longer canine teeth than any other predator. One of these teeth is at least 10 times longer than the biggest tooth in your mouth. Using its big canine teeth and its broad, powerful jaws, a tiger can kill its prey with one quick bite.

1

2

Like other cats, tigers usually keep their claws hidden beneath their fur *1*. This way the claws do not wear down too quickly and won't make noise when the tiger steps on rocks or hard ground. When it wants to use its claws for grabbing or scratching, the tiger extends them *2*.

Tigers are strong enough to d huge animals a long way. A si tiger can pull a water buffalo weighs more than a ton. It wo take more than 12 men to mo such an enormous weight.

QUESTION: How is a tiger's face like your thumb?

ANSWER: The stripes on the tiger's face are like a thumbprint. No two people have exactly the same thumbprint. And no two tigers have exactly the same stripe pattern.

The tiger at left is similar to one of the three pictured below. Is it Tiger *1*, Tiger *2*, or Tiger *3*? (Hint: Look at the stripes above the eyes and on the forehead.) You'll find the correct answer printed upside-down below.

Correct Answer: Tiger 3.

1

2

3

It takes a lot of muscle to move a 400-pound body. A tiger's body is packed with muscle. It can leap 10 yards over level ground, or jump 15 feet in the air. It can move so gracefully that it doesn't make a sound.

Tigers are big-game hunters. They hunt water buffalo, wild pigs, deer, and other large animals. The Bengal tiger, below, is about to attack a gaur that may weigh a full ton.

Tigers are also big eaters. In a single year, one tiger must eat about 70 deer or other large animals. That is one reason why tigers hunt alone. If they lived in big groups, they could never find enough prey to feed them all.

Many people think that a big, dangerous tiger could easily kill all the prey it wanted, but that's not true. The life of this big-game hunter isn't easy. Most of the animals it tries to attack get away. A tiger sometimes goes weeks without eating. When that happens, it may hunt animals that can be dangerous even for a tiger.

To get enough food, tigers have to hunt day and night. They often hunt at night, when deer and antelope are most active. Tigers also hunt at night because they are safer from humans then.

Tigers cannot run fast for long distances so they must get close to their prey before attacking. On their huge, padded feet, they can creep silently to within 20 feet of another animal without being heard. This tiger is ready to leap. Notice how its rear legs are pressed beneath it, like a pair of giant springs about to be released.

When it hunts, a tiger usually sneaks close to its prey by hiding behind trees, bushes, and rocks.

Then, in a series of explosive leaps, it attacks from behind. This tiger springs to attack a young tapir.

Next, the tiger grabs its prey with its claws and pulls it to the ground. It bites the animal on the throat or on the back of the neck to kill it.

Tigers and other predators play an important role in nature. By killing deer and other prey, they keep the numbers of these animals under control. Because of this, the animals that survive are healthier.

If there were no tigers in the wild, the number of prey animals would grow too fast. At first, they would eat so much that they would destroy many plants. Then, many of these animals would go hungry.

A big, hungry tiger can eat about 100 pounds of meat at one sitting. This is about one-fifth of its total weight. That would be like a 10-year-old human eating 40 hamburgers in one meal. A tiger has to eat a lot because it often goes several days without eating anything.

On occasion, a tiger attacks a baby rhino. This can be dangerous, because the mother rhino is probably nearby. Even a tiger does not want to anger a 4,000-pound rhino!

The tiger drags its prey into the brush. What it cannot eat, it buries to save for another meal.

If a tiger is hungry enough, it may even attack a bear. That may be a big mistake. This Siberian tiger has attacked a Eurasian brown bear that is almost twice its size. The bear is also stronger than the tiger and every bit as mean.

Tigers usually live alone. But they sometimes meet other tigers. When they do, you never know what will happen next. Male tigers may fight over a female or over a hunting territory. Then again, they may just share a meal, or walk away peacefully.

When male and female tigers meet, they may spend a lot of time playing, like these two Sumatran tigers in the water. Playing is a part of their courtship, and sometimes the play is rough. At other times, male and female tigers treat each other very gently.

Their ways may be mysterious to us, but tigers seem to communicate well with other tigers. And tigers have many different ways of sending messages.

Every tiger has a private hunting territory. It also has several ways of warning other tigers to stay out. It may mark the borders of its territory by scratching trees (left), or by leaving a scent. When one tiger recognizes the smell of another, it always makes a funny face (above).

Tigers are solitary but sometimes sociable. Most socialization occurs at kills. Males don't help to raise their offspring, but they sometimes share a kill with females and cubs.

A male tiger may even encourage cubs to eat from the kill while he waits his turn. One male tiger was seen to wait for hours, until cubs and tigress had their fill, before he ate.

The male and the cubs greet each other in typical tiger fashion by rubbing heads, shoulders, sides, and nuzzling faces.

When a tiger wants to share a kill with other tigers, it sends out a signal. Its roar can be heard for 1½ miles. Other tigers that hear the roar will come and share the food. When a tiger doesn't want to share its food, it may growl or snarl.

ROAR

ROAR

ROAR

When female tigers roar, they may simply be trying to attract a mate. As you see here, male and female tigers are not always rough with each other. They can be quite gentle.

Very few cats like the water, but tigers love it. They often lie in shallow pools to cool off, or to get away from flies and mosquitoes. They also love to swim and play in water, like children in a swimming pool.

Sometimes tails do all the talking when tigers meet. An upright tail that wags slowly back and forth says, "Hi, I'm friendly." A tail that lashes rapidly from side to side says, "I'm excited!" And a lowered tail that twitches from side to side says, "Watch your step."

FRIENDLY

EXCITED

TENSE

Baby tigers look like cute kittens. At birth, they are about 12 inches long, and they weigh less than 2 pounds. In a year's time, these "kittens" will be big enough to hunt deer and buffalo.

A mother tiger usually gives birth to two, three, or four cubs at a time. This is necessary so that at least one of her cubs will survive. Many predators attack tiger cubs. To help keep them safe, the mother may stay with her cubs for about two years. During this time, the young tigers have a lot to learn from her if they are to hunt and survive on their own.

Like all young animals, cubs are full of energy. They spend their days wrestling, chasing each other, and darting after butterflies. All this exercise helps to prepare them for their first real hunt. They are ready to begin hunting at about six months, but they will continue to depend on their mothers for food until about 18 months of age.

SIBERIAN TIGER CUB

It's hard to believe that in just six months, this playful little cub will be a ferocious hunter. By then, it will weigh almost 200 pounds and will have four big canine teeth for attacking prey.

A female tiger is one of the most loving and caring mothers in the animal kingdom. She cuddles her babies to keep them warm. She feeds them and protects them from enemies. She teaches them how to hunt and survive in the wild for two years or more, when they leave her to find their own hunting ranges.

This cub is only a few weeks old. In the wild, cubs are usually born in caves and other protected places. The mother keeps them there and brings them food for two or three months. After that, the cubs are big enough to follow her as she hunts for prey.

INDIAN PYTHON

The life of a baby tiger is filled with danger. If a mother leaves her cubs, even for a short time, predators may attack them. Some of the animals that like to eat tiger cubs are leopards, pythons, and hyenas.

STRIPED HYENA

LEOPARD

13

These people are not hunting tigers. They are visiting a wildlife reserve in India, where they can see tigers in their natural habitat. With a walkie-talkie, the guide can pass information about the tigers to game rangers and other guides.

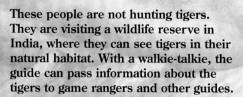

Ancient Indian legends and sculptures depict the tiger as a symbol of power. In Asia, people have always thought of the tiger as "the king of beasts." This is a major reason why the demand for tiger parts is so great in Asian markets.

People admire tigers. This is not surprising, because tigers have many of the qualities people admire most in animals.

Tigers are strong, beautiful, intelligent, graceful, and independent creatures.

But people who live in tiger country not only admire tigers— they also fear them. Some people claim that tigers kill many humans. Although we know this isn't true, it may explain why so many tigers have been hunted and killed by people.

There are still some places in the world where we can see tigers living in the wild, if we are lucky. Today, it is illegal to hunt tigers. But even in preserves, poachers kill tigers.

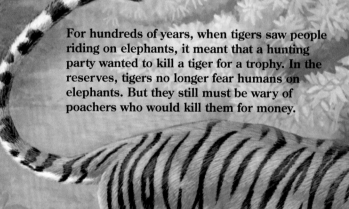

For hundreds of years, when tigers saw people riding on elephants, it meant that a hunting party wanted to kill a tiger for a trophy. In the reserves, tigers no longer fear humans on elephants. But they still must be wary of poachers who would kill them for money.

Many tales have been told about ferocious tigers killing people. Few tigers actually kill humans. Those tigers that do are usually too old, sick, or weak to catch their natural prey.

Even something as small as a porcupine quill could cripple a tiger, making it too slow to hunt other animals. Then, if it got hungry enough, it might attack a person.

Tigers now do the hunting amid the ruins of Ranthambore—once the royal hunting park for the maharajahs of Jaipur. Ranthambore is one of several former princely hunting preserves that have become national reserves to protect tigers and other wildlife.

Hunting tigers used to be sport for royalty and the wealthy people of India. But tiger hunts weren't sporting, because the tigers had little chance to escape. The hunters rode on elephants, while their servants (called beaters) noisily drove the tigers toward the hunters. Over the years, many thousands of tigers were killed this way.

The few wild tigers remaining in the world can only be saved with a lot of hard work—and perhaps it's already too late. These majestic animals once ruled the forests of Asia, but there may be only 5,000 of them left. The Caspian, Java, and Bali tigers are already extinct, and very few of the south China tiger remain.

When it became illegal to hunt tigers, it seemed that the greatest threat to tigers was the destruction of their forest habitat. And for many years that was true. In the forests of Asia, bulldozers and chainsaws are busy. More than 80 percent of India's forests have been destroyed for lumber, firewood, and to clear land for farming. Habitat loss continues to be a problem, but illegal hunting, or poaching, now kills the world's tigers.

During the early years of Project Tiger, an ambitious program that began in 1973, wilderness preserves were established where tigers would be protected. And, indeed, the numbers of Bengal tigers increased. In more recent years, the demand for tiger bone and other tiger parts in the medicinal markets of China, Korea, Taiwan, and Southeast Asia has made a dead tiger worth a lot of money to a poacher.

Dedicated people around the world are working hard to improve the tiger's uncertain future. They work to establish more reserves, to teach people who live near tigers how to manage the land and still leave habitat for tigers, and they work to see that existing laws to protect tigers are enforced. Additionally, they try to teach a larger Asian culture that tiger parts will not cure all ills.

Protection and education programs cost money. We can all help by donating to funds that purchase habitat for tigers, by supporting the work of scientists and conservationists who try to save the tiger, and by learning all we can about tigers and other endangered animals. To learn more about how you can help, write to:

World Wildlife Fund
1250 24th Street NW
P.O. Box 97180
Washington, D.C. 20090-7180
www.worldwildlife.org